CW00480878

35 MORE GREAT CHILDREN'S LESSONS

THAT BRING THE BIBLE TO LIFE

Special Thanks To:
God for guiding my steps and for my wife and son who put up with my missteps

PARENTING BOOKS BY MARK J MUSSER

50 Great Object Lessons that Bring the Bible to Life

50 More Great Object Lessons that Bring the Bible to Life
When it comes to explaining the Bible to children and pre-teens, many parents and even Sunday school teachers are at loss as to how to really connect their children or students to God's Word, bringing it to life in interesting and creative ways. Thankfully, 50 Great Object Lessons makes it incredibly easy!

Lessons on Parenting: What Parents in the Bible Can Teach Parents Today
The Bible is full of insightful and meaningful narratives where Moms and Dads are found making choices that impact their children and those around them. The blessings or fallout from those choices and decisions most definitely can apply to our lives as parents today.

The Christ Centered Home: Turning Your Kids into Christ-Centered Disciples
Long before God established the nation of Israel to be His chosen people, and long before He established the church to spread His glory, He established the family to be the primary means of making disciples. Is your family fulfilling that mandate?

Parenting Essentials: 10 Things Every Parent Should Do
Do you know what you should be doing as a Christian parent? Do you understand what essential characteristics must be modeled for your children and teens? These are the questions this family-defining book seeks to answer.

OTHER BOOKS BY MARK J MUSSER

Answers for the Afterlife: The Truth about Heaven and Your Place in It
Is there life after death? If so, where is it and how do I get there? These questions leave us uneasy. Instead of living in assurance, we spend our days doubting the afterlife or wondering where we'll end up when we die. But we can be sure. Are you?

World Changer: Impact the World for Christ Starting Now
Do you want to be a world changer, impacting our planet one needy soul at a time? This book will inspire you to make a difference and step beyond the ordinary. Don't miss your chance to leave a legacy for Christ. Don't miss the adventure of a lifetime.

Finding the True You: Discover Who You Were Created to Be
"Who am I, and what is my purpose?" If you are looking for the answers to these foundational questions, download a copy of this book today!

Searching for More: Finding the Fulfillment You Long For
The answers to fulfillment and satisfaction are not found in anything this world has to offer. They are found in Christ alone. Discover what you're missing!

"A BOOK THAT TACKLES THE CONTEMPORARY AND THE CONTROVERSIAL WITH TRUTH AND GRACE."

The Hills of Vincere Ridge

Life is anything but easy for fourteen year-old Jason Collins. Adopted and raised by a same-sex couple, his standard school day consists of lingering stares, not-so-subtle whispers, and outright bullying. His only escape, hours of quiet solitude working on his golf swing. Then one weekend, hearing the words of Jesus--*Come to me all of you who are weary and carry heavy burdens, and I will give you rest*--Jason comes, trusting those words to prove true.

Life, however, gets infinitely more difficult. While his moms struggle with his decision to trust Christ, a publicity seeking pastor manipulates the teen into petitioning for new legal guardians, setting off a firestorm of protests, picketing, and media baiting.

Enter TJ Lanter, a former professional golfer still working to overcome his own tragic past. Together, the two fight to use their shared loved of golf to create a bond that enables both to see through their pain and discover that Jesus does indeed embrace the weary and give them rest.

AVAILABLE NOW ON AMAZON.COM!

TABLE OF THEMES

INTRODUCTION

God's plan from the beginning has been incredibly simple. The current generation of Christians must teach the next generation of Christians what it means to follow Christ. Then, when that generation grows up, they will turn around and do the same for those who follow.

That is the purpose of this lesson book. Let it be a tool in your hands to help disciple and train the next generation to live for, and serve, Jesus Christ. Whether it be in your home, in Children's Church, Sunday school, Pioneer Clubs, AWANA, tweens ministry, or some other avenue, I pray God will work mightily through you!

Each lesson is broken down into the R.E.A.D. F.F. formula. The "R" stands for READ. Right at the beginning of each lesson, you will share a Scripture passage with the children.

"E" stands for ENGAGE. Here you will share a short story or anecdote.

What follows is "A" where you will ASK a series of questions designed to get the children to think about, and interact with, the lesson and the Scripture.

"D," for DO, comes next. Here is where you work to etch the lesson onto the hearts and minds of those in your care as you go through an object lesson, craft, or exercise together.

The final two "F's" stand for FOLLOW UP and FINISH UP. As you near the end of each lesson, you will follow up with questions and application ideas to check on what has been retained and to encourage the children to put into action what they just learned about.

Finally, you will finish up with a time of prayer.

As a parent or teacher, God has called you to the great task of discipleship. Grab hold of that responsibility and watch as the Lord does awesome things in and through you!

Well, what are you waiting for? Let the adventure begin!

LESSON 1

SUPPLIES
A special treat or surprise you know the kids would like; a set of directions to that treat

READ: Psalm 119:104-106

ENGAGE
Gary's dad was *not* very good at remembering directions while driving. Some people can drive to a place once and then always remember the way. Gary's dad, however, was *definitely* not like that. Once he even made a wrong turn coming home from church, and he'd gone that way hundreds of times before!

For Gary's father to make it anywhere without any problems, he needs to have the directions with him in the car. When he has those trusty directions plugged into his phone, he doesn't have any problems. But when he forgets the directions...well, let's just say Gary knows it's going to be a loooong and frustrating drive!

Traveling through life is kind of the same way. God's Word is our directions for life. If we remember to keep His Word close to us, we will get to where we need to be. But, if we forget to keep God's Word close...well, that can be really frustrating too!

ASK
Has your family ever gotten lost driving somewhere?

Why is it always good to have directions with you when driving, especially if going somewhere you've never been before?

How is the Bible like directions for us to travel through life?

Do you make sure to read the Bible every day? Why is that important?

What is God's Word called in verse 105? Why do you think it is called that?

What are some things that can help you remember God's Word?

DO

- **Before class:** Hide a bag of candy, five dollars, or something else you know the children would enjoy finding. (Make sure whatever was hidden will *not* be found without directions)
- Create a set of directions that lead to that hidden prize
- Make sure the directions read similar to below
  - Move twenty feet forward, turn right at the door
  - Walk forward eight feet, go left at the red chair
  - Slide under the table six feet. After standing, make a slight left at the yellow lamp, etc.
- Give the children the map and let them seek out the "treasure"

FOLLOW UP

Ask: Do you think you would have found this prize without the directions?

Discuss how God's Word is a lot like those directions. The Bible will lead us to the best life possible and provide us with wisdom, guidance, direction, hope, peace, and so much more.

Discuss the importance of reading the Bible. Talk about a time period each day that would work for each one to spend time in God's Direction Book.

FINISH UP

- Thank God for His Word which is our directions for life
- Ask God to remind you to keep His Word close to your heart

FUN EXTRA

If doing at home, have the kids hide something and create a set of directions for *you* to find.

If doing in a classroom setting, encourage your class to hide something at home for their parents to find using directions they create. Ask them then to discuss with their families how God's Word is like directions for life!

LESSON 2

SUPPLIES
Several sheets of paper; markers; scissors; tape

READ: Joshua 1:7-8

ENGAGE
Sarah had a big math test coming up and knew she needed to study, but then her best friend called and invited her over. That sounded like way more fun than studying for a math test, so she went to her friend's house. The next day, Sarah did *not* do well on her math test.

Meanwhile, Leslie also had that same math test coming up. Yes, her favorite TV show was coming on, but she knew studying for the math test mattered more. So, she turned off the TV, spent time studying, and got a great grade on the test!

Like Sarah and Leslie, we have the choice to study or not to study for school. AND, we also have the choice to study or not to study the Bible. When we study the Bible, it usually leads to passing God's tests. When we don't study it, well, that usually leads to not doing so well on God's tests.

ASK
What do you like, and not like, about tests?

Studying for tests is important, but sometimes it is easy to get distracted. Likewise, studying God's Word—the Bible—is very important. But what things tend to distract you from reading the Bible and spending time with God—Could it be friends, TV, video games, internet, etc.?

What did God say would happen to Joshua if he didn't get distracted and was sure to study and obey the Bible?

The devil likes to distract us so that we won't ever read the Bible. Why do you think he does that?

What can we do to make sure that the devil doesn't distract us from what's really important?

DO
- **Before class:** Line up 12-15 sheets of paper end to end,
- Tape the ends together, creating a narrow pathway about twelve or thirteen feet long
- Just at the arm's reach of a child, on either side of this path, place other sheets of paper that have words written on them like—TV, INTERNET, VIDEO GAMES, SPORTS, DOLLS, COOL TOYS, and other things that might interest your kids (or class)
- After you have finished the last question above, have the kids line up on one end of the narrow pathway
- Ask them, one at a time, to walk down the pathway while trying to collect the papers to their left and their right. (You should place these papers in such a way that it will be very difficult to collect them without falling off the pathway)
- After each child has gone down the path, place any papers that may have been picked up back in their spots
- After every child has gone through, fold the "path" in half long-ways, so that it is half as wide as before. Ask the children to go through again, doing as they had done before

FOLLOW UP
Ask: Was it difficult to stay on the path while trying to pick up the papers?

Remind the children how the Lord told Joshua that if he stayed focused on God's Word, the path, and didn't go off to the left or right, things would be good for him. Discuss how the papers to the left and right of the path caused some to fall off, or almost fall off, the path.

Finish by talking about how there are many distractions that will try to get us away from studying the Bible or following God's path, but we need to do our best to ignore those things and stay focused on what the Lord has for us.

FINISH UP
- Thank God for His Word which He gives you to study
- Ask God to remind you to read His Word often and learn from it
- Ask God to help you not be distracted by the devil

LESSON 3

SUPPLIES
A space to play follow the leader

READ: 2 Timothy 4:6-8

ENGAGE
Gym class was coming up and Johnny knew that he and the rest of the fifth graders were going to have to run "the mile." He was *not* looking forward to it. The last time he had to run the mile, he almost threw up! That certainly wasn't fun.

Nevertheless, in gym class, Johnny lined up for the run along with the rest of his class. Most everyone was groaning, and they hadn't even started running yet! Suddenly, the gym teacher blew the whistle and they were off.

Some ran a little bit and then just started walking. Others stopped altogether, hunching over and gasping for breath, but Johnny and a few more kept going hard. They were keeping their eyes on the finish line where their teacher was clapping and cheering them on.

It seemed like it was taking forever, but Johnny did it! He crossed the finish line. He finished the race!

ASK
Do you like running? Why or why not?

What hard things have you had to do in gym class? Were you able to do them?

Why is it Important to finish what you start?

In our Bible verses, did Paul finish the race that He was running for Jesus? How did he do?

What do you think it means to "run the race for Jesus"?

What can help you keep living for Jesus throughout your whole life?

DO
- Tell the children that you are their leader and they have to follow you during a race. The only way to win the race is to do exactly as the leader does
- Inform the children that you will not SAY what you are doing, so they will have to watch you closely and follow what you DO
- Have the kids follow you around an area you have designated as you hop, jump, crawl, run, fly with arms out, etc.
- Continue to play as time allows and change "leaders" so that others have an opportunity to lead as well

FOLLOW UP
Ask: What was the hardest thing you had to do in order to keep following the leader?

State, "Following the leader and finishing the race wasn't always easy, but everyone could do it IF they kept their eyes on the leader." Discuss how Jesus is our leader and we can best live life on earth by keeping our eyes on Him.

Finish by talking about how reading the Bible, praying, going to church, and listening to parents are great ways to always help us know what our leader, Jesus, is doing.

FINISH UP
- Thank God for people who encourage you to live for Jesus
- Ask God to strengthen you to always live for Him
- Ask God to help you always follow your leader, Jesus

LESSON 4

SUPPLIES
Can of dark soda (*Sprite* or *7up* won't work); clear glass that will hold the full contents of the soda; two or three ¾ to one inch-size buttons

READ: Psalm 32:1-5

ENGAGE
Jeremy was feeling guilty and feeling guilty was making him miserable! Playing baseball outside one Saturday, he accidently hit a ball right through the dining room window while his parents were out taking a walk. When they came home, he told Mom and Dad that a bird had flown into the window. He even made the lie seem more believable by finding some bird feathers and putting them on the dining room floor.

His lie actually worked. His parents believed him, and he wasn't in any trouble at all! But he couldn't stop thinking about it. Every time he walked into the dining room, the guilty feelings came back. When he heard his mom telling a neighbor the story, again those feelings rushed in. Yes, indeed, he was miserable!

Finally, Jeremy confessed. Yes, he got in trouble for the window *and* for lying, but he felt *much* better inside.

ASK
When you know you have done wrong, how do you usually feel inside?

According to our Bible verses for today, how do we feel when we don't confess our sins?

What happens when we do confess them according to verse 5?

Why is it important that we pray and ask God for forgiveness?

Why is it also important to confess it to your parents as well?

Do you need to ask forgiveness for anything?

DO
- Pull out a clear glass cup and state that the glass represents our lives
- Pour dark soda into the glass and explain that the soda is the dark place deep inside our hearts where we like to try to hide our sin
- Talk about how we all do bad things, say bad things, and think bad things. Instead of confessing them, sometimes we try to hide what we have done
- As you finish saying the above, grab the buttons and state that they represent the bad things you just talked about
- Drop the buttons into the glass. They will sink to the bottom effectively out of sight
- (The buttons will stay at the bottom for a few seconds.) Move on to say that even though we think we have hidden our sins, they have a way of popping back up. (The buttons should rise to the surface)
- Go on to note that we may try to hide them again (thrust a finger down onto a button on the surface and it will disappear again for a few seconds), but those sins just keep coming back to make us feel guilty all over again. (Button should rise again to the surface)[1]

FOLLOW UP
Ask: What's the problem with trying to hide sin?

Discuss how confessing our sin is the only way to get rid of the sin, as well as getting rid of the guilty, miserable feelings that sin causes.

Remove the buttons from the soda and finish by encouraging the kids to be sure to confess any sins, instead of hiding them. The only way to keep them from showing back up is to get rid of them!

FINISH UP
- Thank God that He is always ready to listen to you pray
- Ask God for forgiveness for any sins you may be trying to hide

LESSON 5

SUPPLIES
Half sheets of regular or construction paper; markers or colored pencils; scissors

READ: 1 Thessalonians 5:17

ENGAGE
Ted was a quitter. If he was playing a board game and losing badly, he would quit. If he could not get by a level on a video game, he would quit. If he was playing games outside with his friends and his team was losing, he would quit. If he didn't get to be king first while playing foursquare on the school playground, he would quit.

Once Ted begged his parents for a whole week to sign him up to play tackle football, but before the first practice was over he quit, saying it was too hot to run around with a helmet on. Are you getting the picture here? Ted was a quitter.

Unfortunately, when it comes to praying, we can all be like Ted. Sometimes, we will pray for someone or something for a couple days, but when we don't see anything happen we quit praying.

Sometimes, also, we can ask God to do something for us. But if God doesn't do it within a couple days, we quit praying about that too.

But you don't want to be a quitter, do you?

ASK
What were some of the things that Ted quit?

Have you ever quit anything? If so, what?

How about prayer? Have you ever started praying for something, or someone, and then quit praying when it seemed like nothing was happening?

What does our Bible verse say about this?

Why should we never ever stop praying?

There was once a man named George Muller who prayed fifty-two years for a friend to accept Jesus. Why is it so awesome that George would pray for someone that long?

Make a list of people you can start praying for:

DO
- **Before class:** Cut sheets of paper or construction paper in half, then fold each half-sheet in half to create "prayer cards"
- After finishing the last question above, hand out the cards
- On the front panel of the "card" have the class write, or help them write if necessary, "Never Stop Praying ~ 1 Thess. 5:17"
- On the three remaining panels, have each child write the name of a person they can pray for (whether it be an unsaved person, someone who is sick, a missionary, etc.)
- You may wish to come with a list of a few people in case the children cannot think of anyone
- After a name is written in each of the remaining panels, allow the kids time to decorate each panel, perhaps in a way that reflects what they are praying about for each person
- Examples: A cross for someone who needs salvation; a hospital bed or bowl of soup for someone who is sick, a Bible for a missionary, etc.

FOLLOW UP
Instruct the children to take their cards home and put them somewhere that will help remind them to pray—on the refrigerator, on the kitchen table, on the nightstand next to their bed, etc.

Finish by reminding each child of the importance of always praying and never quitting on prayer, even if it seems nothing is happening...for fifty-two years!

FINISH UP
- Thank God that He answers all prayers in His perfect time
- Pray for the people you listed under the last question
- Ask God to remind you to never give up on praying for someone or something

LESSON 6

SUPPLIES
A large button; a piece of fabric at least six inches square; sewing thread; needle

READ: Jonah 1:1-3

ENGAGE
Nine year-old Jeremiah has a little poodle named Kobie. A couple months ago, Jeremiah's family found out that their tiny ten pound dog has diabetes, which means Kobie needs to get a shot *twice* a day with a special medicine that will help him stay healthy. HOWEVER, the shots can be painful!

When Kobie sees Jeremiah's dad coming at him with the needle, he runs and tries to hide! Of course, that little dog doesn't know enough to understand that what is in that needle is meant to help him. And, in fact, his life is *much better* when he gets the shot compared to when he does not get the shot.

Now, we humans should know better, but we all can act like Kobie when it comes to God. We know that God has what's best for us. But instead of coming to Him and praying, we go off and do our own thing. I bet the whole time God is thinking, "It would be so much better if they would just come to Me!"

ASK
Have you ever seen someone trying to give medicine to a pet (or maybe a baby) who didn't want it? What were you thinking when that happened?

What did God want Jonah to do?

What did Jonah do instead because he didn't like what God said?

Why is it a bad idea to try and get away from God when He has so much good for us?

If God asked you to do something you didn't like, why should you still say "YES"?

What do you do each day, and each week, to help you stay close to God?

DO

- Get out the piece of fabric and large button
- Tell the kids that the fabric represents God while the button represents us
- Put the button on the fabric and try to walk around with it a couple of times, allowing the button to fall off each time
- Say, "Boy, if this button is us, and the fabric is God, then we are sure having a hard time staying close to God as we go through life. What's the problem here?"
- The kids should answer that the button is not attached to the fabric
- Congratulate the children for the right answer and begin using the needle and thread to quickly sew the button on
- Walk around once more with the fabric and button[2]

FOLLOW UP

Ask: Why did the button stay on that time?

Discuss with the kids how life can be difficult, but it is a whole lot easier when you stay close to God.

Talk about ways that each of us can stay close to God—through devotional times, prayer, church attendance, kids clubs, listening to Christian music, hanging out with Christian friends, etc.

FINISH UP

- Thank God for all the great things He has for you
- Ask God for the strength to do what He asks you to do
- Ask God to help you stay close to Him, even if what He seems to be asking you to do is hard

LESSON 7

SUPPLIES
Small pieces of paper with "YES" written on them, one small piece of paper with "NO" written on it, fun-sized candy bars equal to the amount of "YES" papers, one king-sized candy bar

READ: Psalm 143:1-6

ENGAGE

George and Gina were bummed. They had been praying for a whole month that their parents would buy them a puppy. And here they were more than thirty days later, but still no puppy! At the dinner table that night, the two eleven year-old twins were just pushing food around their plates and barely speaking. Dad picked up on this right away, "What's wrong with the two of you?"

George started in, "Well, we've been praying like forever for a puppy, and God didn't give us one yet. It's not fair that He's not answering our prayer!" Gina nodded in agreement.

"Interesting," Dad smiled. "Do you think that God only answers prayer with 'yeses'? Can't He also answer prayer with 'no's' or 'not yets'?" George and Gina squirmed a bit in their seats. "Remember, God will do what He knows is best for *everyone* when the time is right. He doesn't just do what *you* think is best as soon as you want Him to."

George and Gina didn't really like Dad's answer, but they knew he was right.

ASK

What were George and Gina praying for?

How long had they been praying for this puppy?

Why were they upset at the dinner table?

What is something that you have prayed for but didn't get the answer you wanted?

Why doesn't God always say "yes" to every prayer?

In our Bible verses for today, King David was praying but life still wasn't easy for him. Did he give up on God and stop praying?

What did he do to remind himself that God was still good even though the answer to his prayers were "no" right then? (See verse 5)

Why should you not give up praying, even if God doesn't answer the way you want Him to?

DO

- **Before class:** Have several small pieces of paper equal to the amount of children in the class (or in your home)
- Have fun-sized candy in a bowl that the class can see, but do not allow any of the kids to see the king-sized candy bar
- Write "YES" on all but one piece of paper and fold them up. Write "NO" on the last piece of paper and fold it up
- After finishing the last question above, inform the children that you will be playing the part of God today and you plan on answering their prayer requests for them
- Hand out the sheets of paper, making sure they know NOT to open them up. Tell them that these sheets of paper have the answer to their requests
- Have the kids line up, making sure the one with the "NO" is last in line, then have the class move toward you one at a time
- When the first child gets to you, take the "request" and open it up, show this child that the answer is "YES!" Rejoice with the child and then give him or her a fun-sized piece of candy
- Go through each of the children with the remaining "yesses." Rejoice with each one and give each a fun-sized candy

- When the last child comes up, open the request and reveal the "NO"
- Say, "Wow, I am sorry the answer is 'NO.' That is a real bummer that you can't have a fun-sized piece of candy. But, hey, that's all right. I have something better for you!"
- Give this child the king-sized candy bar[3]

FOLLOW-UP

State that when God says "NO" to things, it is usually because He has something much better in store for us.

Ask: For example, what are some reasons God might be telling George and Gina that they cannot have a puppy right now? (Answers could include: God knows the family will be moving soon and a puppy would be difficult to take care of during such a transition. God knows money may be tight in the future and the extra expense of caring for a pet will be too much. God knows George and Gina may not be ready for the responsibility, etc.)

Discuss how even when an answer is "NO," we can trust that God *always* does what is best for us. We can know, without any doubt, that He will always give us what we need when we need it.

FINISH UP

- Thank God for answering prayers how He knows is best
- Ask God to give you patience to wait for His answer
- Ask God to help you trust Him even when the answer is "NO"

LESSON 8

SUPPLIES
PART 1—Two backpacks filled with heavy objects (or two safe, heavy objects to carry like medicine balls); space to have a race or obstacle course

PART 2—Plain shoeboxes or other small, plain boxes equal to the amount of kids in the class (or home); scissors; sheets of paper; markers

READ: Matthew 11:28-30

ENGAGE
As Roger walked home from school, he couldn't stop thinking about his dad who was very sick and in the hospital. He tried to think about other things—happier things—but every thought went back to his dad. And if that wasn't bad enough, his book bag was extra heavy that day.

The longer he walked, the heavier it felt. By the time he got home, his back and shoulders were aching. Mom, who was watching, decided to use that book bag to teach a lesson. "That book bag was heavy, wasn't it?" Mom asked, "You probably wish you had someone who could have carried that for you, don't you?" Roger nodded.

"Well," Mom continued, "I know you have a heavy weight thinking about your dad too. But you don't need to carry that burden. You can give it to Jesus and let Him carry it for you."

Roger knew his mom was right. "Okay Mom, I understand. Can we pray right now?"

ASK
Why was Roger sad and feeling down?

Besides his dad being in the hospital, what else was bothering Roger?

What are some things that you worry about sometimes?

What should you do with these things that worry you?

Do you always let Jesus carry your worries and your hurts, or do you just try to carry them yourself? Why is it always better to let Jesus carry them?

Do you have any worries or hurts you need to give to Jesus right now?

DO—PART 1
- **Before class:** Find a space to do a relay race or create an obstacle course
- After finishing the last question above, have two lines of children competing against each other. The first two in each line will put on the heavy backpacks (or be given a heavy object to carry)
- These first two in each line will run to a designated spot (or go through the obstacle course) and come back, handing the backpack (or object) to the next person in line
- After everyone has had a chance to go, run the race again *without* the backpack or heavy object

DO-PART 2
- **Before class:** Cut slits in the tops of each box you collected for class. Make sure each slit is wide enough for sheets of paper to easily fit through
- After finishing the race or obstacle course, hand out each box and tell the children that these are "burden boxes." Whenever they feel burdened by a problem or a worry, they should write down a prayer to God and put it into the box, allowing the Lord to take care of it
- Have the children write "Burden Box" on their box and decorate it as they wish with Bible verses, pictures, etc.
- When they are done, have them write down one prayer request on the slips of paper you have provided and place it in their boxes[4]

FOLLOW UP

While the children are working on their burden boxes, ask: When we did the race, was it easier to run with the backpack on or off? Why?

Discuss how it is easier to go through life when we are *not* carrying burdens. Talk about how the burden box is a great way to give our burdens over to God, so that we can go through life without being weighed down.

FINISH UP

- Thank Jesus for His willingness to take your burdens
- Give Jesus any hurts, worries, or burdens you have

LESSON 9

SUPPLIES
A blindfold for every child in the class (or home); fifteen to twenty balls or other items that can be strewn on the floor

READ: Psalm 119:1-3

ENGAGE
Twelve year-old Mitchell was excited to be able to sleepover at his buddy Kevin's house. It was going to be epic because there would be five or six other kids from his grade there too!

However, at that sleepover, after the adults went to bed, Kevin pulled out a BB gun and told all the kids to sneak outside so they could take turns shooting at his neighbor's porch light.

Mitchell sure didn't want to do that, but he also didn't want to look uncool. So he said to himself, *"I'll go outside with them, but I won't shoot the BB gun."* Though, when someone handed him the gun, he grabbed it. This time he said to himself, *"I'll shoot, but I'll make sure to purposely miss."*

Guess who was holding the gun when Kevin's neighbors looked out their window!?!

Sometimes we make compromises so that we can look good in front of others. But God is never pleased when we follow our friends instead of following Him.

ASK
At the beginning of our story, why was Mitchell really excited?

What caused Mitchell to not be so excited anymore?

Can you think of a time that you did something you should not have done because you didn't want to look bad in front of your friends? What was it?

What should Mitchell have done differently?

What do our Bible verses say about how God's people should act?

What can help remind you to follow God and not follow your friends or others?

DO
- Gather the kids around and say you are going to play a game of follow the leader, only everyone is going to be blindfolded
- Move all the children to one end of the room and place blindfolds on all of them. Once the blindfolds are in place, scatter fifteen to twenty balls, or random objects, between the kids and the "end line"
- Choose one of the blindfolded children to be the leader. It is that child's job to lead all the others from one side of the room to the other without stepping on all the "hazards, perils, and dangers" that stand in their way
- Allow the leader to try to get everyone safely from one side to the other. (If time permits, allow other children to be the leader as well)
- After it becomes obvious that "the blind cannot lead the blind," inform the class that you will guide everyone through
- Give careful instructions to guide everyone from one side to the other without making contact with any of the objects

FOLLOW UP
After removing all the blindfolds, ask: Which was better? Being led by someone in a blindfold or by someone *not* wearing a blindfold? Why?

Discuss how we humans do not know and understand everything, and we certainly cannot see the future. But God does know and understand everything; He even knows the future! Because He sees everything clearly, He can best guide us through life.

Talk about times when we may want to follow our friends who want to watch something bad, go to inappropriate websites, play Rated-M video games, take a candy bar from a store without paying for it, etc. We may be tempted to go along with our friends who can't see the bad things that could happen because of those choices. In those times, we need to remember to follow God's Word which tells us not to do certain things because the Lord sees all the negative things that can happen because of wrong choices.

FINISH UP

- Thank God for people who help you make good choices
- Ask God to remind you to always follow Him, even if your friends don't want to

LESSON 10

SUPPLIES
Internet access. If internet access is not available, you can download the Youtube video in the DO section onto your laptop or tablet before class using www.keepvid.com. You may also screenshot a page from www.operationworld.com noted below and have it handy for the lesson

READ: Isaiah 49:1-3

ENGAGE
Like many people, Austin Gutwein loves basketball. Unlike most, however, Austin has used his love for hoops to raise *millions of dollars* for AIDS orphans in Africa. At age ten, Austin decided to get people in his community to sponsor him in a free-throw shooting event. He shot 2057 free-throws (because that's how many children are orphaned due to AIDS each day), and he raised over $3,000 for *World Vision*, enough to help eight orphans.

But Austin wasn't satisfied. The next year, he got 1000 others to join him shooting free-throws and raised well over $100,000. The third year, Austin decided that he wanted to do a specific project, so he raised enough funds to build a school in Zambia. In the fourth year, all those free-throws brought in over $200,000 for a medical testing center.

Now, more than ten years later, Austin still keeps doing great things to raise money to help people and show them Jesus' love!

ASK
What sport does Austin really like?

How did he use his love of basketball to make a difference for Jesus?

Austin was just ten when he started doing this. Do you think you could do something like Austin did, even though you are young? Why or why not?

What does God say to Isaiah in verse 3?

What great things could God do through you if you let Him?

DO
- Show a short three minute video of Austin. Go to YouTube and search "Austin Gutwein - Hoops of Hope – RightNow"
- Go to www.operationworld.org. There you can click on any country, get prayer suggestions, and learn how you can best pray and help different parts of the world

FOLLOW UP
Ask: You see that there are *a lot* of needs all around the world, aren't there? What do you think we can do about this?

Discuss things your class may be able to do to make a difference. Perhaps adopt a class from an inner-city public school and raise school supplies for them, find ways to provide supplies or Bibles to a homeless shelter or detention center for youth, make cards for shut-ins, sing at a nursing home, etc.

Encourage the kids to show their parents www.operationworld.org and make a pledge to pray for a different country each day.

FINISH UP
- Thank God for His plan for you and for His world
- Pray for a country of the world
- Ask God to use you to make a difference in the world

LESSON 11

SUPPLIES:
Paper and directions to make a paper airplane (You can go to www.foldnfly.com to get these directions); space to fly paper airplanes

READ: Leviticus 26:1-5

ENGAGE
Sarah really wanted to go to the zoo on Saturday to see the new baby panda bear that had just been born there. In fact, she wanted to go so badly that she spent the whole week begging her mom.

Mom said, "If you do all your chores this week, get all your homework done without complaining, and don't have any attitude problems, we will go to the zoo."

That sounded great to Sarah and she agreed. However, Sarah did *not* do all her chores, "forgot" about some homework, and had a couple episodes of attitude. So guess what? Sarah's mom did not take her to the zoo.

Meanwhile, Sarah's brother Stanley really wanted to go see the *Titanic* exhibit at the Franklin Institute. Dad said, "Do your chores, get your homework done, and keep the attitude in check and we will go."

That sounded awesome to Stanley, so he made sure to be on his best behavior, and guess what? He got to go see the *Titanic* exhibit and loved it!

God is much like Sarah and Stanley's parents. He wants *very much* to bless us and provide for us. However, to receive the fullness of that blessing, He asks that we show our love for Him by listening and obeying.

ASK
What did Sarah really want to go see? Why did she end up not being able to see it?

What did Stanley really want to go see? Why was he able to go and experience it?

Can you think of something you really wanted to do, but didn't get to do it because you got in trouble? What was it?

In verse 3, what did God say the people must do to experience His many blessings?

How well are you doing at obeying God?

How well are you doing at obeying your parents?

DO

- Have a sheet of 8.5x11 paper and your paper airplane folding directions out
- Tell the kids you are going to show them how to make a cool paper airplane and then you all can enjoy the fun of seeing how it flies
- With a quizzical look, check out the directions and say these look complicated and you think you can do it better without the directions
- As you go through the directions, keep saying, "It says (fill in a direction), but I think I will do this instead."
- In the end, you want to finish with a "plane" that could not possibly fly any real distance at all
- After your "plane" collides to the ground, talk about how "not fun" that was and wonder aloud what went wrong
- Allow the kids to answer that you did not follow the directions
- Close this section working together to all make paper airplanes by carefully following the instructions
- Take turns flying your planes

FOLLOW UP

Ask: How did it go when I didn't follow the instructions that the creators of the website provided me? How did it go when we all did follow those instructions?

Discuss how just as the website creators know the best way to make a paper airplane, so God, as our creator, knows just how to make it so we have the best life possible.

Talk about how the paper airplane folk gave instructions so we could have the most fun flying planes. Likewise, God, our creator, gave us instructions so that we could experience a blessed life (not a perfect, or even easy, life but a blessed one).

State: "When I didn't follow the instructions for the airplane, it was not so good, and I was missing out on what a great paper airplane could do. And when we don't follow God's instructions, it's not so good either. We end up missing out on a lot of the good stuff the Lord has for us."

FINISH UP
- Thank God for all the blessings He has waiting for you
- Ask God to help you live in obedience to Him by following the instructions He has given in His Word

LESSON 12

SUPPLIES
Check out (and even print out) kid friendly volunteer ideas (one such list is found at www.signupgenius.com/nonprofit/kid-friendly-volunteering.cfm); an intact apple; a knife

READ: Leviticus 19:9-11

ENGAGE
Hey, want to hear about some world records? Let me throw a few at you: Sonya Thomas set a record by eating 8.5 pounds of sausage in just ten minutes! Don Lerman hit the record books by eating six pounds of baked beans in one minute and forty-eight seconds. Gross!

Meanwhile, Takeru Kobayashi ate fifty-eight Johnsonville Brats and 17.7 pounds of cow brains (eww) in ten minutes. And, not to be outdone, Joey Chestnut ate sixty-eight hotdogs (and their buns) in ten minutes, and later, ate 103 Krystal Burgers in eight minutes. I think his tummy will hurt tomorrow!

These records show a WHOLE LOT of eating, but did you know that in some places in the world many kids have to go without food? In fact, I am sorry to say that *twelve* children around the world die of starvation every minute. That, certainly, is no good.

I wonder if by the end of this lesson, we can come up with some ideas to help lower that number!

ASK
What are some of the things that people were eating *really* fast?

What is something that you think you could eat really fast?

In our Bible reading, what does God say to keep in mind when getting food for yourself?

Why is it important to remember that there are people in need all around the world?

What could you give or donate to the less fortunate this week?

DO

- Pull out an apple and cut it in half down the middle
- Inside an apple, you will generally find between two and five seeds. Pull these seeds out and show them to the kids
- State that each of those seeds could be planted to create a whole new apple tree
- Ask: Who knows how many apples an apple tree will produce in its lifetime?
- State that an apple tree can produce up to 200 apples a season for as many as twenty years. Meaning, in its lifetime, an apple tree can produce up to 4000 apples!
- Multiply the number of seeds you have by 4000. For example, if your apple has four seeds in it, tell the kids that your apple could make up to 16,000 more apples!

FOLLOW UP

State: You may be wondering what this has to do with our lesson, but think about this. We know that there are *lots* of people who are starving. Millions and millions of them! Because that is such a *big* number, we might think, "What can I do about that? I'm just one little ole person." But guess what? If these four tiny seeds can make up to 16,000 apples, then our little class (or family) could do *big* things too!

Discuss how if you planted those tiny little seeds in the ground, you would start to see *big* results in a few years. But if you didn't plant them, then you shouldn't expect anything. Likewise, if we don't do anything about the problems we know about, then we shouldn't expect anything to change. But if we start to do even little things, change will happen!

Take out the list of kid-friendly volunteer ideas and talk with your class (or family) about what you can do to be different makers!

FINISH UP

- Thank God for all the many things that He has given to you and blessed you with
- Ask God to remind you to always give back to Him
- Ask God to show you what you can do to make a difference in the lives of those who need help

LESSON 13

SUPPLIES
A picture of a million dollars in ones or twenties; a picture of a billion dollars in ones or twenties

READ: Mark 10:17-22

ENGAGE
Eight year-old Jimmy was super excited. His family had just pulled into the Chuck E Cheese parking lot, and he was ready for a great Saturday of playing games and winning tickets. Practically before his family even found a place to sit down inside the restaurant, Jimmy was off to skee-ball.

The little boy expertly rolled the ball up the ramp and landed it in the center circle several times. He did so well that, after just five games of skee-ball, he already had 220 tickets! But even though he was getting lots of tickets at that game, Jimmy grew bored with it and ran off to the ball-drop. Incredibly, he managed to get the ball to drop into the bonus hole three times and earned another 275 tickets! He was definitely on a roll!

By the end of the day, this young Chuck E Cheese fanatic had amassed over 1200 tickets! Incredible! Jimmy happily took those 1200 plus tickets to the prize counter and traded them *all* in for fifteen tootsie rolls, a jolly rancher ring, and two rubber bracelets. It was definitely a great day for Jimmy.

The next day, Sunday, Jimmy's dad gave him his allowance and reminded him that he needed to put some of it in the offering at children's church. After church, however, when Dad asked Jimmy how much he put in the offering, Jimmy said, "Oh, I forgot to put some in."

There was silence for a moment or two, then Dad said, "You know, yesterday you gave up *all* your tickets for a few little things and some candy. Today, you had a chance to give up just a bit of your money to bless the church and help others, but you didn't give anything."

Jimmy didn't say anything, so Dad continued, "You might think that what you got yesterday is worth a lot, but what God can do with what we give Him is worth a whole lot more."

ASK

Why was Jimmy so excited on Saturday?

How many tickets did Jimmy earn while at Chuck E Cheese? What did he do with them all?

The next day at church, Jimmy got his allowance and was told to make sure he put some in the offering, but what did Jimmy do?

What did Jimmy's dad say about this?

In our Bible story for today, what did Jesus tell the rich young man he needed to do if he wanted to experience eternal life?

How did the rich young man respond?

The rich young man thought the stuff he had was better than what Jesus had for him, but why is what Jesus has for us always better?

If you had a chance to talk to Jimmy, or the young man from our Bible story, about their decisions, what would you tell them?

DO
- **NOTE:** The following includes a discussion about one million dollars vs one billion dollars. Since small children don't comprehend large numbers well, show them the pictures of how much one million dollars looks like compared to how much more one billion dollars looks like
- Pointing to the picture of the one million dollars, ask: Would you rather

have one million dollars to spend in a week or (pointing to the one billion dollars) a billion dollars to spend over your *entire* life?

- Most would choose the billion to have for a lifetime, but you could talk about how it would be fun to spend a million dollars in a week—buy a big house, lots of nice toys, go on a great vacation to Hawaii, etc. It would be a great week, but then it would be over
- Talk about how the house you bought would start to need repairs, the toys would break or get boring, the vacation would just be a memory
- Meanwhile, the billion for a lifetime would always be there. (Point to the picture of the billion again), that is *a lot* of money to have for your whole life. Yup, that is way better than a million!

FOLLOW UP

Say: You might be asking what this has to do with our lesson today. Well, here it is. Jesus is like the billion dollars that is with you for a lifetime. Meanwhile, all the stuff we have here with us now is like the million for a week. Sure, video games, toys, TVs, etc. are fun for a while, but then they break, get boring, rust, or something else.

Go on to discuss how Jimmy got some candy and some little prizes that he will probably forget about in a couple weeks, and the rich young man got to go home to all his stuff, which won't last too long either. Meanwhile, both had opportunities to give to Jesus but didn't do it.

Talk about how Jesus loved us so much that He gave up *everything* for us to leave Heaven and come to earth, and then even died on the cross for our sins.

Ask: How can we always make sure that we give our all back to Jesus and keep Him first in our lives?

FINISH UP

- Thank Jesus for giving up everything for you
- Confess to God, if necessary, choosing stuff over Him
- Ask God to strengthen you to use all your time, talents, and treasure for His glory and the benefit of others

LESSON 14

SUPPLIES
Bag of fun-sized candy (optional); note cards for each person in the class; colored pencils or markers

READ: Job 41:11; Psalm 50:10-12

ENGAGE
After a busy Saturday doing chores, Dad decided to take his six year-old son, Jeffrey, out to McDonalds for some lunch. Dad, being hungry from all his chores, ate up his burger and fries pretty quickly. Jeffrey, however, was eating much slower and had plenty of fries left by the time Dad finished.

So, reaching over, Dad grabbed for one of the fries on Jeffrey's tray. Jeffrey was not pleased with this! Shouting, "HEY!" he covered the rest of the fries with both hands.

"What?" Dad started, "You can't share?"

"These are MINE!" Jeffrey shouted again, not thinking about the fact that he only got to McDonald's because his dad took him, and he only had fries because his dad bought them.

Because of this, Jeffrey was told that, for the rest of the lunch, he would eat what he paid for, and Dad would eat what he paid for.

Jeffrey did not like this new plan!

Sometimes, when it comes to God, we can be like Jeffrey. We forget that everything we have comes from Him. So when He asks us to tithe our money or give to missionaries, we should remember that it is *all* from Him and then be more generous with what He has given us.

ASK
What wouldn't Jeffrey share?

What did Dad think about this?

What "plan" did Dad put in place to teach Jeffrey an important lesson?

What lesson was it that Dad was trying to teach?

How well do you share the stuff God has given you?

What do our Bible verses say that God "owns"?

Why does God want us to share with Him when He has everything already?

What are some things your family can share with others this week?

DO
- **Before class** prepare each note card. Using colored pencils or markers, in vibrant letters, write out something similar to--"You're great. I hope you have an awesome day!" on each
- After finishing the above questions, get out the bag of fun-sized candy and give each child three to five pieces
- And/or also hand them each the note cards you have prepared

FOLLOW UP
State, "Just like God provides us with great things and many blessings, so I gave each of you some candy and an encouraging card. You didn't do anything to earn it. I just gave it to you because I love you and wanted to share with you."

Ask: How does it feel to have someone share with you?

Discuss how God shares with us so that we will learn to share with others. State, "Just like I shared with you, now you need to practice sharing with others."

Instruct the children to give their note cards to another person as an encouragement. If you also handed out fun-sized candies, have them also share all but one piece with others

FINISH UP
- Thank God for sharing so much with you
- Ask God to help you be generous with what He has blessed you with
- Ask God to give you opportunities to share this week

LESSON 15

SUPPLIES
A small cardboard box; scissors, a large piece of candy (or several coins)

READ: Luke 12:13-21

ENGAGE

Greed. Do you know what word means? Well, the dictionary basically says that greed is "wanting money or power too much." This reminds me of King Midas. Have you heard of him?

King Midas, the story goes, was so greedy for money that he prayed for the power to turn everything he touched into gold. Amazingly, his prayers were answered! Soon, everything he touched turned to gold, and he was becoming richer by the second. He thought this was the greatest thing ever!

However, soon he was hungry and decided to eat. But when food touched his lips, it turned to gold. He could not digest anything! His daughter, seeing her father dying of starvation, rushed to him to give him a big hug. But upon touching him, she, too, turned to gold.

What King Midas thought would be so incredible turned out to be not so incredible after all. Sometimes, the same can be true for us as well. We think that if we just had more stuff life would be better, but God never designed stuff to make us happy. And usually focusing on stuff, instead of on God, just makes life a lot harder.

ASK

If you, like King Midas, could have one prayer answered, what would it be?

King Midas thought his prayer being answered was amazing at first, but then it wasn't so amazing anymore. Why not?

In our Bible story for today, there was a brother who was much like King Midas.

What does Jesus say to this brother, in verses 15 and 21, who wanted part of his father's property?

What do you think Jesus was trying to say to this man?

What are some things that you really like and spend a lot of time with?

Do you sometimes focus on these things too much? If so, what can you do about this?

DO

- **Before class:** Place the large candy bar (or coins) in a box, seal it up, and then cut a slit in the top of it that is wide enough for you to stick your hand in but not wide enough for you to pull your hand out when it is balled into a fist
- After finishing the above questions, pull out the box and tell the kids that there is a fantastic prize inside. Shake the box so they can here it rattling inside
- Inform the class that you are going to get it out because you *really* want it. Stick your hand inside, and smile widely as you grab hold of it. Let the children see how excited you are to have it in your hand
- With the candy clenched in your fist, attempt to remove your hand from the box
- Try several times and appear upset that you can't get your hand back out with it wrapped around the candy bar
- Finish by explaining that you can only get your hand back out if you release the prize

FOLLOW UP

State, "Did you know in some parts of the world that hunters will catch monkeys with something similar to this box? Yes, they will make a trap and put the monkey's favorite fruit inside. Then they will drill a hole in the trap big enough for the monkey's hand to fit in but not big enough for the hand to come out when it is holding the fruit. Even when humans come around to catch it, it will refuse to let go of its favorite fruit and will stay trapped.

Discuss how your hand was trapped inside the box so long as you tried to hold onto the prize. Similarly, the devil tries to trap us by getting us to love stuff like video games, movies, TV, the internet, money, etc. too much. Even when something is bad for us, sometimes we still won't give it up.

Further share how we can also be trapped when we are so distracted by these things that we miss out on all that God has for us. None of the stuff we have in our homes or rooms will matter when we die, but whatever we do for the Lord will last forever.

FINISH UP
- Thank God for how much He loves and cares for you
- Ask God to help you build a strong relationship with Him
- Ask God to help you not focus on temporary stuff so much, but to focus more on the things that will last forever

LESSON 16

SUPPLIES:
Twenty-one small, square, stackable children's blocks. If you do not have those, twenty-one plastic cups will also work

READ: Luke 21:1-4

ENGAGE
Jenna was an average teenager who liked to spend her money like most teen girls do—on make-up, magazines, clothes, shoes, and an occasional purse. If you asked her, she would have told you that she loved Jesus and wanted Him to be first in her life. However, most of her choices seemed to show that she was first in her life.

That is, until her youth pastor challenged her to really start living for Jesus.

Soon God led her to a homeless shelter that desperately needed supplies like soap, toothpaste, mouthwash, and more for the people they ministered to. Jenna thought, "This is my chance to surrender."

On her birthday, she decided to NOT ask for any birthday presents. Instead, she told everyone to use the money they would have spent on presents to buy products for the homeless, then she would take them to the shelter.

ASK
What was the best birthday present you have ever received?

What would you like to get as a present for your next birthday?

Instead of getting that present for your next birthday, do you think you could do something like Jenna did? Why or why not?

How is what Jenna did like what the widow did?

Why did Jesus say that the widow gave "more" even though she actually gave much less than the others?

DO

- **Before class:** Place the twenty-one blocks in a pile in one corner of the room
- After finishing the last question above, tell the children that before you continue you want to stack the blocks in the corner into a pyramid that goes 6, 5, 4, 3, 2, 1
- Go to the corner where the blocks are and take one at a time to another corner and begin stacking them into the pyramid
- As you do this, be sure to mention how time consuming this is and you're sorry to interrupt the class for so long doing this
- When you finish stacking the blocks, apologize again for taking so long

FOLLOW UP

Ask: What could have made that go quicker?

After the children respond that it would have gone quicker if everyone pitched in to help, state that you want to test and see if that is true.

Tell the kids that the whole class will now work to take the blocks, now stacked in a new corner, and restack them back in their original corner.

Once the job is done, tell the kids that it was indeed much faster when everyone pitched in to help.

Go on to discuss how when you did the work alone, it took a lot longer and wasn't as good as when many hands were involved. This is similar to how it takes longer to help many people when only a few people are working to bless others. But when everyone pitches in to help, then many more people can be blessed...a whole lot faster!

Many children will wonder what they can do being little and not having much. Remind them that the poor widow didn't have much, but Jesus was very pleased because she was willing to give it.

Ask: With that in mind, what can you do this week to pitch in and help others?

FINISH UP
- Thank God for all that He has done for you and for all that He has blessed you with
- Ask God to help you be generous with what He has blessed you with
- Ask God to give you opportunities to pitch in and be a blessing this week

LESSON 17

SUPPLIES:
Some less savory tasting ingredients for baking cookies like flour, baking soda, vanilla extract, raw egg, etc; fresh baked cookies (or chewy store bought cookies)

READ: 1 Kings 17:8-16

ENGAGE
Heather was a three sports' star in middle school, but soccer was by far her best sport. In just sixth grade, she was on the starting squad with eighth graders. With the soccer season just underway, things couldn't have been going any better for her. She scored five goals in her first three games!

But in the fourth game, she collided with another player and cracked one of her vertebrae. She would have to be in a back brace for a year and might never be able to play soccer again. Heather was devastated and thought life was over.

Yet, with all the extra time she had not being able to play sports, she began to read her Bible more and pray. Soon, she was getting closer and closer to God and experiencing joy and fullness in ways she had never dreamed of before.

Yes, what started out as a very bad thing was quickly becoming a *great* thing.

ASK
What was Heather really good at?

What happened to Heather that made her have to stop playing soccer?

What did Heather think right after this happened?

How did God turn this bad situation into a great one?

Have you ever had a bad experience that God turned into a good one? If so, what was it?

The widow and her son in our Bible story were going through a very tough time, what was the matter?

What amazing thing did the widow and her son see God do because they were going through a hard time?

The next time something bad happens to you or your family, what should you remember from this story?

DO

- Have the less savory tasting cookie ingredients handy
- Allow the kids to taste some flour, some baking soda, and/or vanilla extract. (You may even consider cracking a raw egg into a glass and see if anyone is interested in drinking it down!)
- Talk about how all of these things taste quite bad and aren't so much fun to eat, yet when we you put them all together with some other ingredients, what comes out is something very good and tasty
- Pull out the fresh-baked cookies (or, if time permits, mix all the ingredients and bake during class) and allow each child to have one or two

FOLLOW UP

Discuss how, just like we can mix ingredients that don't taste good with some good tasting ingredients to create something very tasty, so God can take our yucky, no fun bad times and mix them with His love and goodness to make something awesome.

Let the kids know that the next time something bad happens to them, their family, or someone they know, they can pray and ask God to mix in His love and goodness to create something awesome from that bad situation.

FINISH UP

- Thank God for being able to turn bad into good
- Ask God to remind you about this story when things get rough
- Pray for anyone going through a difficult time right now

LESSON 18

SUPPLIES:
A clear jar; pebbles; sand; rocks

READ: 1 Kings 19:19-21

ENGAGE
Many people have never heard of C.T. Studd, but he is someone who did amazing things for God's kingdom. C.T. was born to very rich parents way back in 1860. He grew up with the best of everything and was one of the greatest athletes in all of England. As a teenager, he was as famous for the sport of cricket as Stephen Curry is famous for basketball here in America.

With all that C.T. had going for him, he could have easily lived a rich, famous, and comfortable life in England. But when his father died, C.T. gave 95% of his inheritance (around two million dollars in today's money) to missionaries and then went to China to be a missionary himself!

Some people thought he was crazy. But this is what C.T. told them, "Some wish to live within the sound of church or chapel bell; I want to run a rescue shop within a yard of hell."

In other words, he was basically telling people that he was going to do whatever it took, and go wherever necessary, so folks could meet Jesus!

ASK
What were some things that C.T. had going for him while he was living in England?

How great would it be if you were rich and famous?

What would be hard about leaving all that money and fame behind to go where God wanted you to go?

Our Bible story for today told us that Elisha had *twelve* oxen. People with that many oxen in Bible times were considered very rich, but what did Elisha do when Elijah called him to come and follow God?

Elisha turned all his oxen into dinner for the town! This was him basically saying, "I am done with farming. From now on, I am just going to follow God where He leads." Why did it take a lot of courage for Elisha to do that?

Are you willing to go where God wants you to go, and do what God wants you to do, this year? What might make it hard for you to say, "yes"?

DO
- **Before class:** Have the clear jar handy along with three bowls—one bowl filled with rocks, one bowl filled with pebbles, and one bowl filled with sand
- After the finishing the last question above, begin to pour the sand from the bowl into the jar, stating that the sand represents things that are not that important like video games, TV, movies, internet surfing, etc.
- After the sand is poured in, start putting the pebbles in the jar on top of the sand. Explain that the pebbles represent stuff that matters but isn't the most important thing—the pebbles represent time with friends, doing chores, working a job, etc.
- Finally, begin to place the rocks inside the jar, stating that the rocks represent what is most important—that is, the things God put you on earth to do for Him
- **NOTE:** You should have enough sand and pebbles in the jar that all of your rocks will not fit
- Explain that all the time spent with stuff that wasn't so important hasn't made room for what God has for us
- Empty everything out and begin again—this time placing the rocks in first
- Filling the jar in the opposite order than you did the first time will allow everything to fit
- To see a video on how best to do this, go to YouTube and search "Jar Of Life - Put IMPORTANT Things FIRST!"
-

FOLLOW UP

Ask: What happened when I put the sand and the pebbles in first?

Ask: What happened when I put the rocks in first?

Discuss how we need to put what God has for us to do first. Everything else must be second. It would not be so much fun to get to the end of our lives only to find out that we didn't leave room for the things God had for us to do

FINISH UP
- Thank God that He has a great plan for your life
- Ask God to strengthen you to go where He wants you to go and to do what He wants you to do
- Ask God to help you keep Him first

LESSON 19

SUPPLIES:
A twenty dollar bill; a picture of four half gallons of ice-cream; a picture of a video game case

READ: Luke 9:57-62

ENGAGE
Imagine if someone came up to your parents and offered them a million dollars, but they said, "No thanks. That's too much money. We wouldn't know what to do with it all."

Right after that, another person comes up and offers them the biggest mansion you have ever seen, but they say, "No thanks. We have a house already."

You can hardly believe your ears, but your parents still aren't done. When a third person comes up and offers to pay for your family to go on a month long vacation to Hawaii, they say, "No thanks. Hawaii is far away. That plane ride would take too long."

That seems crazy, doesn't it? Who would give up all those great things! Yet, when Jesus calls us to follow the great plan He has for our lives, we usually make similar excuses.

Now, of course, Jesus probably doesn't have millions of dollars, mansions, and Hawaiian vacations in that plan, but you can have no better life than the one that He has planned for you!

ASK
What three things did the people in our story offer your parents?

What would you have said to those people? Why?

What do you think makes a life great?

What did Jesus want the people in our Bible verses to do?

What did they say to Him?

If Jesus asked you to follow Him, what would you say?

What would be hard about leaving things behind to follow Jesus?

DO

- Pull out a twenty dollar bill and say that you need the kids help in deciding how to spend it
- State that you are really hankering for some ice-cream and you know that you could buy four half-gallons of ice-cream (show a picture of four half-gallons of ice-cream) and then eat it all in a day because you love it so much
- Or you could buy a really cool video game that you like (show a picture of the video game). It is usually more expensive but you found it for just twenty dollars
- Finally, you could give the money to support a missionary in Japan who is working to tell Japanese people about Jesus

FOLLOW UP

Ask: What do you think I should do with the money?

Guide the discussion by talking about how fun it would be to eat all that ice-cream in one day. Yet, with the video game, you could play it again and again for many, many, many days. But if you gave it to a missionary, that missionary could lead someone to Jesus who then would be in heaven *forever*.

Ask: What is better? To have something fun for just a day, something fun for many days, or something that lasts forever?

Discuss how the best use of the money is for something that will last longer. From there, talk about how the best use of our lives is for things that will last forever. We could live for here and now, spending all our time with stuff that doesn't last, or we can do the things God wants us to do and those things will last forever.

Finish by talking about things we could do for the Lord like serve others, tell people about Jesus, pray for others, give to missionaries, help at a homeless shelter, send cards to people in the hospital or nursing homes, etc.

FINISH UP
- Thank Jesus for the great plan He has for your life
- Ask God to use you to do great and amazing things
- Ask God to help everyone focus on the things that last not the things that don't

LESSON 20

SUPPLIES:
A sheet of paper for everyone in the class; sharpies; pencils; pens; crayons

READ: Galatians 2:20

ENGAGE
At the age of four, Alexandra Scott and her family moved near Philadelphia to be close to the Children's Hospital there. You see, Alexandra (or Alex as she liked to be called) had cancer and needed to go that hospital often.

At this hospital, Alex learned that many little kids, like herself, were battling cancer. Knowing that something needed to be done to help them all, Alex decided to build a lemonade stand in her front yard to raise money for kids with cancer. Even though her own health wasn't good, she set up her lemonade stand as often as she could. By age eight, Alex, along with others, raised nearly one million dollars!

Unfortunately, it was at age eight that Alex lost her battle with cancer and died. But since then, another thirty million dollars has been raised! It is amazing what one little life can do, isn't it?

And, you know what? When that life is in Jesus' hands, then nothing is impossible!

ASK
In our story, what was wrong with Alex?

Even though Alex's life wasn't very long, why was it still a great one?

What does Paul say about his life in Galatians 2:20?

Did Jesus have control of Paul's life? Does Jesus have control of your life?

What amazing things do you think could be done through you if Jesus had control of your life?

DO
- Give each child a clean sheet of paper. (Make sure something protects the table underneath it or that the paper is thick enough that the *Sharpie* won't bleed through)
- Give each child one pencil, one pen, one crayon, and one *Sharpie* (or other heavy marker)
- Have each child write his or her name on the sheet of paper with each writing implement. Make sure they write their name the same size with each of the four writing implements they received

FOLLOW UP
Ask: Which name shows up more boldly than the others?

Ask: Which one do you think will last the longest if the paper got wet?

Discuss how we are to live our lives like *Sharpies*. We should stand out, live boldly for Jesus, and do great things for Him.

Talk about how a *Sharpie* is a PERMANENT marker. What it writes on, it stays on. Likewise, whatever we do for the Lord lasts forever and leaves a permanent mark on the world.

FINISH UP
- Thank God for being able to do anything
- Ask God to fill your life with Himself
- Ask God to use your class to do amazing and eternal things for Him

LESSON 21

SUPPLIES:
None

READ: 1 Kings 18:16-21; 30-39

ENGAGE
Glenn and four other friends were having a sleep-over party at Jason's house. Late that night, after his parents went to bed, Jason pulled out a DVD movie that had a lot of bad things in it.

After just a couple minutes, another boy, named Richie, told Jason to take that DVD out because it wasn't a good thing to be watching. But Jason and the others told Richie to quit being a "Mama's boy" and man-up. Glenn, meanwhile, just sat there quietly. He knew God wouldn't want him filling his heart and mind with the stuff that was in that movie, but he didn't want to look like a loser in front of his friends. He was frozen in silence.

Suddenly, while Glenn was still thinking about all this, Richie bolted up from the floor and went over to turn the TV off. Jason wasn't going to let that happen. He grabbed Richie by the leg while the others blocked the TV.

Again, Glenn did nothing.

However, as you can imagine, all the commotion woke up Jason's dad, who came stomping down the steps into the living room. "It's after midnight! What in the world is going on?"

Jason immediately let go of Richie's leg. But other than that, no one moved and no one said anything. Looking at Glenn, who seemed to not be part of the commotion, Jason's dad asked, "What do you have to tell me, Glenn?"

Glenn now had a choice. Would he do what was right and tell what happened or stay quiet? Glenn decided it was finally time to do what was right.

ASK

What did Jason do that wasn't very good?

How did Richie react to this?

Even though Glenn felt the same as Richie, why didn't he say or do anything?

If you were Glenn, what would you have told Jason's dad?

In our Bible story, when Elijah told the people to choose between the real God and fake gods, how did the people react? (See verse 21)

What did it take for the Israelites in our Bible story to realize that God is the true God, and they should do what's right?

Have you ever been in a situation where you had to choose between following God and following friends? If so, what was it?

DO

- Take the children through the following scenarios. For each, first ask what they would do, then ask what they think Jesus would do
- You're at the dinner table and everyone starts eating right away, YOU: 1. Start eating right away also   2. Pause and say a quiet prayer to yourself   3. Ask if you can say a prayer for everyone at the table
- You have some free time, so YOU: 1. Spend it all playing video games   2. Spend it all watching TV   3. Spend half with video games and half with the TV   4. Spend some time praying and reading the Bible
- Everyone is ignoring the new kid at school because he seems a bit weird, YOU: 1. Ignore him as well   2. Make fun of him for seeming weird   3. Be nice to him   4. Steal his backpack as a joke
- A friend yells at you and calls you a mean name, YOU: 1. Call your friend some mean names back   2. Vow to never be a friend to that person again

3. Say nice things back to your friend and then pray for him when you get home   4. Tell all your other friends to be mean to that friend
- You broke a lamp because you were running around the house. After hearing the crash, your mom comes in the room and asks what just happened, YOU: 1. Lie and say, "I don't know"   2. Blame the dog   3. Tell the truth and accept the consequences   4. Run and hide
- Feel free to come up with some of your own scenarios as well

FOLLOW UP
Ask: Is following Jesus always easy? Why or why not?

Talk about how following Jesus is NOT always easy, but it IS always the right thing to do.

Ask: What are some things that can be done to help you better follow Jesus?

Finish by discussing how reading the Bible daily, praying often, having Christian friends, regular church attendance, listening to Christian music, etc. can help us all be better followers of Jesus.

FINISH UP
- Thank God for people in your life who are helping you learn to better follow Him
- Ask God to help you always follow Him

LESSON 22

SUPPLIES:
A board; a drill with a power cord. If you do not have such a drill, an object that must be plugged in to use effectively is a good substitute—like an electric can opener, CD player, or pencil sharpener

READ: Psalm 66:1-4

ENGAGE
For her eleventh birthday, Samantha finally got the gift she had been begging for since she was eight years old—an Ipod touch. She tore open the plastic packaging and excitedly prepared to start using it. Only, when she tried to turn it on, all she got was a black screen.

Frantically scanning through the directions, she read, *"This device must charge for at least twelve hours before it can be used."* Doh!

Plugging it into an outlet, Sam anxiously waited until the next day. It seemed to take forever, but, the next day, our birthday gal grabbed her fully charged Ipod and began loading song after song after song onto it.

However, again, after about eight hours...black screen. Sam had drained all the power. It would need to charge up again! Ugh! Technology!

In a lot of ways, we are much like Sam's new Ipod. We aren't much use for the Lord when we are not "charged up," and the only way to get charged up spiritually is to plug into God and His power every day.

ASK
What was Samantha super-excited to get for her birthday?

Even though she absolutely loved this new gift, what was the problem with it?

What kinds of things do you use that need to be charged up regularly?

In our Bible verses for today, the writer is talking about things that charge him up for God. What are some of those things?

What are things you can do to plug into God and charge up?

How often do you do these things? Should you do them more?

DO
- Grab a wooden board and drill (unless you are using another item)
- With the drill unplugged, attempt to drill a hole in the wood. Push down hard on the wood with the drill bit, work to manually spin the bit, etc.
- Act confused and tell the kids that you don't know what is wrong because your drill usually works well at home—see if they can figure out that it is not plugged in
- Once the children realize the drill is not plugged in, plug it in and use it to easily make a hole in the wood

FOLLOW UP
Ask: Which way was easier for me—with the drill plugged in or not plugged in?

Ask: Why was it easier for me when the drill was plugged in?

Go on to discuss how life is much harder for us when we don't stay plugged into God's power source. Trying to live life without God's power is like trying to drill a hole with a drill that's not plugged in.

Finish by talking again about the things you can do to stay connected to God's power source.

FINISH UP
- Thank God that He has all the power you need to live a great life
- Ask God to fill you with His power, so that you can be used by Him to make a difference in the world

LESSON 23

SUPPLIES:
Poster board or large piece of construction paper; old newspapers or magazines; scissors; glue; marker

READ: Psalm 23

ENGAGE
At an elementary school fair, seven year-old Sadie won a goldfish. She proudly brought little "Goldy" home in a plastic bag filled with water. The next day, Mom bought a small goldfish bowl for Goldy, filled it with water, and put it on the kitchen window sill.

Sadie's job, every day, was to sprinkle in some fish-food into the bowl. And, every Saturday, she had to clean out the bowl and provide fresh water for her little pet. Now, Sadie did a great job with her chores. In fact, when Goldy saw her coming every morning, he started swimming to the water's surface because he knew food was coming! Yes, Sadie took care of all Goldy's needs throughout his whole life.

A lot of goldfish only live for a few months, but Sadie did such a fantastic job with Goldy that he lived for almost four whole years!

Did you know that just like Sadie took care of all Goldy's needs, so God takes care of all our needs as we go through life. And just like Sadie, God always does a fantastic job!

ASK
What did Sadie win at the fair?

How did she do at taking care of Goldy?

What would be the good and bad things about having to care for a pet fish?

How does David say God takes care of him in Psalm 23?

What are ways that God takes care of you?

How can you thank God for all He has done for you?

DO

- **Before Class:** Draw a picture of a large fishbowl on poster board or construction paper
- Using wall putty or scotch tape, fix the poster board with the fishbowl on the wall
- After finishing the last question above, tell the children that you will be handing out magazines and newspapers. It is their job to look for pictures of things that God uses to take care of us—things like food, clothes, houses, beds, the sun, rain, crops, fruit, etc.
- When they find such pictures, they are to cut them out
- After several things are cut out, allow the children to take turns gluing the pictures inside the fishbowl

FOLLOW UP

Ask: Alright, what are some things that we have inside our fishbowl? What are some ways that God takes care of us?

After going through the items, discuss how Sadie did a great job taking care of Goldy and God does an even better job of taking care of us.

Finish by talking about ways you can praise and thank God for all the many ways He cares for you.

FINISH UP

- Thank God for being there to take care of you
- Ask God to help you always remember what He does for you

LESSON 24

SUPPLIES:
Blindfold; obstacles

READ: Matthew 6:9-13

ENGAGE
Mom was getting pretty frustrated with little Jackson. Every time Jackson got angry, he would blurt out some words that were not very nice. Because of this, Mom had to talk with her son about this several times as well as give consequences. Even so, Jackson still kept struggling with not saying those words.

Finally, Mom asked, "What do you think God wants you to do about this, Jackie?"

"Say I am sorry and ask for forgiveness," the little boy answered.

"Yes, that is important and you need to do that," Mom started. "But there is also something else you should do. When you start to get angry, you should pause and pray, asking Jesus to lead you away from the temptation to say or do something wrong."

Jackson thought that was a good idea and told Mom that he would try to remember that the next time he got angry.

ASK
What bad thing did Jackson do when he got angry?

What did his mom tell him to do about this?

In the Bible reading for today, after Jesus tells us to pray and ask forgiveness, what does He say next?

Why is it a great idea to pray to be led from temptation?

How often do you pray and ask God to keep you from doing or saying things that are bad?

Can you commit to praying every morning and asking the Lord to lead you from temptation and bring you closer to Him?

DO
- Ask for a volunteer who is willing to be blindfolded and then try to walk from one side of the room to the other without hitting any obstacles
- After the blindfold is on this child, you can set up chairs, or even use other children, to be obstacles.
- Be sure to make it virtually impossible for the blindfolded person to get from one end of the room to the other without bumping into something
- Guide the blindfolded child to one end of the room and have him or her try to get through the obstacles to the other side of the room. Offer no assistance
- When the first volunteer proves unsuccessful, allow for other volunteers as time permits. (Be sure to rearrange the obstacles for each person)

FOLLOW UP
Ask: How difficult was it to get from one end of the room to the other without hitting an obstacle?

Discuss how trying to get through the obstacles blindfolded is like trying to get through a day without relying on God

Talk about how when we wake up each morning, we cannot possibly see the temptations and troubles that we will encounter throughout the day, but God already knows all about them. Because of this, we need to pray every morning and ask God to lead us from temptation and guide us safely through the day

FINISH UP
- Thank God that He has the power to keep temptation from overwhelming you
- Ask God to lead you from temptation and deliver you from the evil one

LESSON 25

SUPPLIES:
None

READ: James 1:22-25

ENGAGE
Mom was heading out to run some errands when she told eleven year-old Reggie to clean his room and set the table for dinner. The last thing Mom heard as she walked out the front door was Reggie saying, "Okay Mom, I heard you."

However, an hour later, when Mom came home, Reggie's room was NOT clean, and the kitchen table was NOT set. Instead of doing any of the things his mom had asked of him, Reggie just played video games.

Needless to say, he was about to be in some trouble!

Like Reggie, we often HEAR our parents and teachers give us instructions, but we don't always OBEY those instructions. Sometimes we even do that with God. For example, we know that the Bible says not to lie, but we do. We know the Bible says, listen to your parents, but we don't. Yes, there is a bit of Reggie in all of us.

ASK
What did Reggie's mom ask him to do?

Reggie said he would do what his mom told him to do, but did he?

Are you sometimes like Reggie—you hear the instructions but don't always obey them?

What do our Bible verses say about this?

Why is it important to listen to AND obey your parents?

Why is it important to listen to AND obey God?

DO
- Play the game "Jerusalem-Jericho"
- Have all the kids stand up and face you. When ready, explain the game as follows:
- Jerusalem is where the Israelites built God's temple, the place where people raised their hands to praise the Lord. So every time I say "Jerusalem," you need to raise both arms high in the air like you are praising God
- In the Bible, we also can learn about the city of Jericho. This city had its walls come tumbling down when God defeated it with a great miracle. So when I say "Jericho," you need to bring your hands down at your side
- Now, here are the final rules to this game. If I say "Jerusalem" but you don't put your hands up, you will be out. And if I say "Jericho" and you don't put your hands down, you will also be out. Also, if you do the opposite of what you are supposed to do, you will be out as well
- After these instructions are given, slowly go through some practice rounds
- As you move from the practice rounds into the elimination rounds, slowly pick up the speed in which you say "Jerusalem" or "Jericho"
- Vary it by saying one or the other a few times in a row. You may even wish to raise your hands when saying "Jericho" and/or lower your hands when saying "Jerusalem" just to add difficulty
- The last person left is the winner
- Play several times if time permits

FOLLOW UP
Ask: What was the most difficult part of this game for you?

Discuss how it was easy to hear the instruction, but not always so easy to do. Sometimes, as the teacher, you went too fast for the children; sometimes you said one thing but did the opposite motion; etc. Similarly, in life, it is often easy to know what our parents or God wants us to do, but not always so easy to do it.

Finish by talking about how practice makes perfect. The more your class would play Jerusalem-Jericho the better everyone would be at it. Likewise, the more you practice following through on what you hear, the better you will get at that as well!

FINISH UP

- Thank God for His Word which guides our lives
- Ask God to help you not only hear and read the Bible's instructions but to obey those instructions as well
- Ask God to help you listen to, and obey, your parents

LESSON 26

SUPPLIES:
Pillows, sponges, Styrofoam balls (and/or other very lightweight objects); weights (or other heavy objects)

READ: James 1:13-15

ENGAGE
Nine year-old Randy and his dad were watching a TV show called *Bacon Paradise*. This show was all about restaurants that only sold food made with bacon. There was a bakery that sold every dessert you could think of, and each dessert had bacon—bacon brownies, bacon chocolate chip cookies, bacon pecan pie, bacon banana bread, and more.

Another restaurant sold something called a "bacon bomb." It was a giant hunk of meatloaf wrapped in FIVE POUNDS of bacon! Randy thought this was the greatest thing ever because he loved bacon so much. Randy's dad, however, did not like bacon at all. Though, if everything was made out of ice-cream that would have been a different story for Randy's dad. Ice-cream was definitely his weakness!

Did you know that just like we have different food weaknesses, so we also have different weaknesses when it comes to sin? What tempts you may not tempt someone else. Therefore, it is important to know where your weaknesses are, because you can bet the devil knows!

ASK
What kind of TV show were Randy and his dad watching?

Why did Randy like this show, but his dad did not?

What is your favorite kind of food?

What do our Bible verses say lead us into temptation?

What happens if we let temptation win, according to the Bible?

Do you know where you are weakest and most easily tempted to do wrong?

DO

- Tell your class that you feel like you are a bit weak and not that strong. In order to gain strength, you know that you need to start lifting weights
- Pull out your lightweight items one at a time. For example, pull out the pillow and say that you think it would be smart to start with that, then lift it a few times over your head
- Ask: How many times do you think I'll need to lift this before I start getting big muscles?
- After the children inform you that a pillow won't get the job done, pull out the next items. For example, pull out two Styrofoam balls. With one in each hand, start doing arm curls
- Ask: Okay, how about these? How many times do you think I'll need to lift these before I start getting big muscles?
- Again, after the kids inform you that foam balls won't work to build muscle, pull out a third, and perhaps even a forth lightweight item, asking the same question each time
- Finally, grab the heavy object, and ask if that is what's necessary to get the job done

FOLLOW UP

Ask: Why do think that the _____ (whatever the heavy item was) will help me build muscle and not the other things I had?

Discuss how only heavy things can help you work hard enough to build muscle and overcome weakness.

From there, move on to a discussion about how we also need to do hard work to overcome spiritual weakness and temptations. Watching TV, playing video games, surfing the internet, etc. won't help us. We need to do the hard work of praying when tempted, memorizing Bible verses to think about when tempted, having the courage to get away from people and things that tempt us, and more.

Finish by talking about what everyone can do this week to build some spiritual muscle in order to avoid falling into temptation.

FINISH UP
- Thank God that He is strong enough to keep you safe
- Ask God to give you strength to overcome temptation
- Ask God to help you put in the hard work to develop spiritual muscle

LESSON 27

SUPPLIES:
A picture of a shiny fishing lure (or an actual shiny lure); fishing pole (if you don't have one, or can't borrow one, you can make one out of a stick and string); gummy worms; five dollar bill

READ: Luke 4:1-13

ENGAGE
(Show the shiny fishing lure.) Do you know what this is? It is called a "lure." It is called that because it's designed to lure unsuspecting fish onto it so they can be caught and eaten for dinner.

Fishing lures are used by fishermen because they are shiny and made to look like the food that bigger fish eat. The big fish gets attracted to it, and once it takes a bite, it's caught on a hook. Because fishermen spend a lot of time studying fish, they know just what kind of lure works best for each kind of fish they want to catch.

For example, a wise fisherman knows that, if you want to catch a bass, you would use a lure that looked like a big worm or one that has lots of colorful, spinning threads. Whereas with trout, crafty fishermen know that a lure with a shiny gold or silver plate will work best.

Much like a fisherman studies fish to know what lure is needed to catch just the right kind, so the devil studies us. He knows just how to "lure us" to make bad choices.

Because of this, we need to be careful of the devil's lures. Getting on his hook is not a good thing!

ASK
What is a fishing lure?

How do fishermen know what lure to use?

Do you like fishing? Why or why not?

In our Bible story for today, the devil was working to lure Jesus into sinning. How many times did the devil try to lure Jesus?

What did Jesus do each time the devil tried to lure Him in?

How can knowing and reading God's Word help you when you are tempted?

DO

- Get out a fishing pole and talk about how the devil is always trying to lure us into sinning and making bad choices
- Put a gummy worm on the fishing hook and dangle it over the children. (Make sure the hook is not sharp or just tie the gummy worm to the fishing line.)
- With the worm dangling above the class, state that this is what the devil is always doing to us. All day long he is trying to get us to go after things
- Take the worm off and put on a five dollar bill. State that if one thing doesn't work, the devil will just try something else
- Dangle the five dollar bill over the children
- Pull the rod back and say that if that didn't work it would just be another thing and then another, until he found the one that worked

FOLLOW UP

Talk about how, in the Bible story, the devil tried to lure Jesus three different ways. Review those three ways.

Remind the children that Jesus was able to resist the devil and his lies by knowing the truth of God's Word. We need to read the Bible every day so that when the devil tries to lure us with his lies, we can know the truth.

Finish by encouraging your class to spend time in the Bible and devotions each day.

FINISH UP
- Thank God for the truth of His Word which fights Satan's lies
- Ask God to remind you to read His Word EVERY day

LESSON 28

SUPPLIES:
One pitcher of cool water; one pitcher of lukewarm/warm-ish water; a cup for every child

READ: Revelation 3:15-20

ENGAGE

Ten year-old Tyler loved the snow. Whenever it snowed, he would be outside building snow forts, snowmen, and begging for snowball fights! Then, afterwards, Tyler would come inside and warm himself by a fire with a nice big cup of hot cocoa. That sounds like a good day, doesn't it?

But can you imagine if Tyler was outside playing in the cold and snow, and, when he came inside, someone gave him a glass of milk that had been sitting on the counter all day? That would taste nasty!

Or how about this? Imagine Tyler just spent the day playing outside under a hot July sun. He comes in for a cold cup of water, but his mom says, "That glass of water has been on the counter all day. Why not drink that?" That would be crazy. Who wants lukewarm water!?!?!

Well, just like we wouldn't want lukewarm milk or lukewarm water, so God does not want lukewarm Christians.

ASK

What did Tyler like to do when there was snow outside?

What do you think is the most fun thing to do when it is snowing?

Have you ever tasted a lukewarm drink? How did it taste to you?

In our Bible verses for today, what does Jesus say about lukewarm Christians?

Why do you think Jesus REALLY doesn't like it when we say we are Christians but don't live like it?

What in your life might need to change so that you are not a lukewarm Christian?

DO
- Provide each child a cup and tell them that there is nothing better on a hot day than a nice, refreshing cup of cool water
- Taking the pitcher with the lukewarm water, pour some into each cup and have the kids take a drink (**NOTE:** To ensure that the water is lukewarm by this point in the lesson, you will need to initially pour semi-hot water into this pitcher)
- After the kids show their displeasure, have them pour the remainder of their drinks back into that pitcher
- Explain that lukewarm water doesn't taste very good and is not very refreshing
- Say, "Let's try this again." Grab the pitcher of cool water and pour some into each cup. Allow the children to sip again

FOLLOW UP
Ask: Now that you have had a taste of both, which one tasted better and was more refreshing?

Discuss how, as Christians, we should act and speak and live in a way that is beneficial and helpful to the world around us. However, when we sin, when we are mean, rude, hurtful, etc., that is not beneficial. This kind of behavior pushes people away and makes Jesus not very pleased with us.

Finish by talking about what Christians can do to be like cool, refreshing water and not lukewarm water

FINISH UP
- Thank Jesus for loving you and caring for you
- Ask God to show you what in your life needs to change
- Ask God to make you like cool, refreshing water for a thirsty world

LESSON 29

SUPPLIES:
Large cereal bowl; water; ground pepper; liquid soap

READ: Colossians 3:1-4

ENGAGE
When twelve year-old Janey woke up on Saturday, she was really excited. Her mom told her that she wouldn't have any chores that day, and she could do whatever she wanted—within reason.

Well, first Janey decided that she didn't even want to get out of bed until nearly 11 a.m. Then she had a little food, took a shower, and got on the computer. The twelve year-old spent a couple hours checking the websites of her favorite bands and chatting online with friends.

After that, Janey turned on the TV and watched a movie followed by a couple TV shows. By now, it was dinner time, so she had dinner with the family and then got back on the computer to catch up again with friends and surf the web.

Soon, it was bedtime. When Janey crawled into bed, she realized that she spent *a lot* of hours with the computer, the TV, and with friends online, but she didn't spend a single minute with Jesus.

ASK
In our story, why was Janey excited about Saturday?

What kinds of things did Janey do with all her free time?

At the end of the day, what did Janey realize she had *not* done?

If you could do whatever you wanted on a Saturday, what would you do?

In our Bible verses for today, what do you think it means when it says, "Think about the things of heaven, not the things of earth"?

How did Janey do at following that verse? Explain:

How are you doing at following that verse? Explain:

DO
- **Before class:** Add water to a large cereal bowl until it is about three quarters full
- After finishing the last question above, place the bowl in the center of your lesson area and state that this bowl of water represents your brain
- Pull out the ground pepper and liberally add the pepper to the water until there is enough black and brown specks to cover a good portion of the water's surface
- Explain that the pepper represents all our thoughts about video games, movies, friends, toys, TV shows, musical groups, sports, etc.—all the stuff of the world
- Finally, pull out the liquid soap and state that this soap represents Jesus and how He can help us focus on the things of heaven—like praying, reading the Bible, being nice to others, telling people about Jesus, thinking about what we learned in church, etc.
- Squirt, or pump, the liquid soap into the exact center of the bowl. (You will just need to squirt for a second or two, or pump twice)
- As soon as the soap hits the water, it will almost instantaneously push the pepper to the edges of the bowl

FOLLOW UP
Ask: Wow! What did Jesus do to all our worldly thoughts?

Discuss how it is not wrong to think about worldly things—TV shows, movies, video games, music, etc. However, when those thoughts fill our brain, it doesn't leave too much room for the things of Heaven.

Talk about how we need to pray often and ask Jesus to push those thoughts aside so that we can spend time thinking about the things of Heaven. Since what we think about is usually what we do, that means if we think about movies, music, video games, then that is what we will spend time with. But if we think about Heavenly things, then we will spend time with those things as well.

Finish up by discussing some good times during the day to focus on Jesus through prayer, Bible reading, listening to Christian worship music, etc.

FINISH UP
- Thank God for all the great things He wants to do in you
- Ask God to help you focus more and more on Jesus

LESSON 30

SUPPLIES:
Construction paper; glue or glue stick; gravel or sand (something hard or coarse); felt or silk-like material (something soft)

READ: James 3:1-5

ENGAGE
In order to get a Cub Scout badge, eight year-old Bryan worked with his dad to plant two trees in the backyard. The trees were young and small, but they were full of leaves and healthy.

Two days later, however, when Bryan went out to water them, almost all the leaves were gone from one of the trees. The little Cub Scout quickly called his dad, who soon discovered that a small (but chubby) caterpillar had been feeding on the leaves.

Dad informed young Bryan that some caterpillars can eat up to 86,000 times their own weight. That is a lot!

Yes, caterpillars are small things, but they can sure do a whole lot of damage. Another small thing that can cause lots of damage is our tongue. It is not a big part of our body, but it can use words to really hurt people if we are not careful.

ASK
What did Bryan and his dad plant?

Why was one of those trees losing all of its leaves?

Caterpillars are small but can cause lots of problems. Our tongues are small as well, but they, too, can cause many problems. Can you think of a time when someone said something mean to you? How did it make you feel?

Someone once said that "sticks and stones may break my bones, but words will never hurt me." Why is that NOT true?

What do our Bible verses for today say about the tongue?

How are you and your family doing at speaking kindly to each other? How can you all do even better?

DO

- **Before class:** Fold a piece of construction paper in half and cut out a tongue like shape. (Folding in half will allow for equal sized "tongues" when you cut)
- On one tongue spread a thin coating of glue and adhere the coarse substance you are using so that the tongue is completely covered. (Sand or ground gravel are good choices)
- On the other tongue spread a thin coating of glue and adhere the soft substance you are using so that the tongue is completely covered. (Felt or a silk-like material is a good choice)
- After finishing the last question above, pull out the two tongues. Tell the kids that the tongue covered in sand is the naughty tongue and the one covered in felt is the good tongue
- Let the children feel both or even allow them to rub "the tongues" against their cheeks
- (If time and materials permit, you can have the entire class make tongues as a craft)

FOLLOW UP

Ask: Which tongue felt nice and soothing? Which one was coarse and rough?

Ask: Can you give examples of when your own tongue was used to be nice and soothing? How about examples of when your tongue was coarse and rough?

Discuss how each of us must work to tame our tongue. God wants us all to use our tongues to help and bless and soothe, not to be mean, rough, and coarse.

Encourage the kids to go home and practice having "good tongues" this week.

FINISH UP
- Thank God for the people in your life who use kind words
- Ask God to help you use your tongue wisely

LESSON 31

SUPPLIES:
Tube of toothpaste; piece of paper; paper towels or wet wipes

READ: James 3:7-8

ENGAGE
Ten year-old Laurie's mom was having some real problems with their pet dog, Silver. It seems whenever Mom put wash on the clothesline to dry, Silver would attack it and pull all the clothes off. Because of this, Laurie's mom developed a plan to teach Silver a lesson.

One day, Mom took a white rag and put it on the clothesline. Every time Silver grabbed at it, she scolded the dog. Finally, after two weeks, Silver seemed to have learned his lesson, so Mom figured it was safe to hang a load of wash on the clothesline and go out and run some errands.

However, when Mom got back, she found ALL the clothes scattered in the yard. The only thing still on the clothesline was the white rag!

Yes, training pets is hard work. It takes time and patience. It is also hard work to train your tongue. It will also take time and patience, but with God's strength you can be known as someone who only uses words to encourage and help others.

ASK
In our story, what problem was Laurie's mom having?

How did Laurie's mom try to train Silver? Did it work?

Have you trained your pet to do something? If so, what? If you don't have a pet, do you know someone who has trained a pet to do something?

What do our Bible verses for today say about our tongues?

Have you been guilty of using your tongue to say bad or mean things?

We can't tame our own tongues. We need God to help us. Since that is true, how can praying to God help you tame your tongue?

DO

- Pull out a tube of toothpaste. State that the tube of toothpaste represents our tongues and the toothpaste inside represents the words our tongues make
- Take out a piece of paper and squeeze out a liberal amount of toothpaste onto the paper
- Say, "Oops, I squeezed out more toothpaste than I wanted to." Ask for a volunteer who can try to put some of the toothpaste back into the tube. (Have paper towels or wet wipes available for the volunteer to use after attempting)
- The volunteer will be unsuccessful since it is impossible to put toothpaste back in the tube, so ask for other volunteers and give everyone who wants to volunteer a chance (time and class size permitting)
- When all the volunteers have had their chance, state, "Well, that didn't work, did it? It seems like it is impossible to put toothpaste back into the tube after it comes out."

FOLLOW UP

Remind the children that the tube represented our tongues and the toothpaste represented the words our tongues make. This means that, just as it is impossible to put toothpaste back in the tube, it is also impossible to take back our words after we have said them.

Discuss how we have to be careful about what we say because words can never be taken back. Sometimes, people remember a mean thing that was said to them for years and years.

Talk about how we need the Lord to help us tame our tongues, so we don't ever have to regret something that we said.

FINISH UP

- Thank God that He is more than able to tame your tongue
- Ask God to go to work taming your tongue so that you can be known as someone who uses words to bless and encourage others
- Ask forgiveness for any mean thing you might have said

LESSON 32

SUPPLIES:
An empty 16 oz bottle of 7up; water; cups; bag of chips; pretzels (Other snacks can be substituted. See below)

READ: James 3:8-12

ENGAGE
Before church on Sunday morning, eight year-old Ben and nine year-old Lizzie were arguing over who was going to get the last pancake at breakfast. During this argument, they did NOT say nice things to each other!

Later, on the way to church, Ben was complaining that Lizzie was looking out his window, and Lizzie was whining because Ben kept touching her knee. It was just one complaint after another for almost the whole ride.

When they finally got into church, Ben and Lizzie did do a great job of worshipping God, singing each song with all their heart. However, once back in the car, they immediately started to fight over which restaurant they should go to for lunch!

Perhaps you can be a little like Ben and Lizzie too. You use your tongue to argue and complain and whine, then also use that same tongue to praise and worship God. That seems weird, doesn't it? How can complaining and worship come from the same place?!?

ASK
How did Ben and Lizzie use their tongues while in church?

When they were not in church, though, what were some of the things that Ben and Lizzie were arguing about?

What do you complain or argue about sometimes?

What do our Bible verses for today say about our tongues?

Should you be using your tongue to complain and argue or to praise and worship God?

What can help you complain less and praise more?

DO

- **Before class:** Empty out a 16 oz bottle of 7up and replace the contents with water. Also, empty out a bag of potato chips and replace with pretzels (or use whatever snacks you have available. Just make sure that what the bag advertises is *not* what is inside the bag)
- After you finish the last question above, pull out the bottle of soda and say that you are really thirsty
- Ask if anyone else is thirsty and would like a little 7up. Pour some out into cups for each child who wants some, then drink a swig yourself
- State, "Whoa! That's not 7up. This is just water! That's a big bummer! Well, at least I have some chips here."
- Grab the bag of "chips," open it up excitedly, only to pull out a pretzel
- Seeming confused, say, "What in the world is going on? First my 7up is water and now my chips are pretzels! Shouldn't I get 7up from a 7up bottle and chips from a chip bag?!?"

FOLLOW UP

Discuss how just as you expect to get 7up from a 7up bottle and chips from a bag of chips, so God expects good things to come from our mouths and not bad things .

Ask some of the children to tell you their favorite drink and their least favorite drink. Go on to say, "How would you like it if you thought you were getting (favorite drink) but it ended up being (least favorite)? You wouldn't like it too much, would you?"

Ask: How do you think God feels when He expects good and nice things to come from our mouths but bad things come out instead?

Finish up by discussing how God wants us to use our tongues to bless, encourage, and be nice to others. He also wants us to use our tongues to praise and worship Him. We all need to make sure the right things come from our mouths.

FINISH UP
- Thank God for the times you get to worship Him
- Ask God to help you use your tongue for worship and praise and NOT complaining and arguing
- Ask God to help you use your tongue to be nice to others not to be mean

LESSON 33

SUPPLIES:
Peanut butter (or other spreadable food); butter knife; one piece of bread; shoes with laces

READ: 1 Corinthians 12:4-7

ENGAGE

Four people agreed to meet at a campground and share a campfire together. The first said he would rent the campsite; the second said he would bring the firewood; the third said he would bring lighter fluid; and the fourth said he would bring the matches.

The first three arrived on time, got the campsite set up, piled the wood, and spread lighter fluid on it. However, the one with the matches never showed up. Frustrated by this, the person who brought the firewood tried to rub some sticks together to create a flame, but that didn't come close to working. In fact, nothing worked.

Without a way to start a flame, there would be no fire.

Did you know that the church is much like this story? God has given each person something special they can do. Each person must do their part for the church, or it just doesn't work like it should.

ASK

What are the things you need if you want to have a campfire?

What is your favorite thing about having a campfire?

In our Bible reading for today, what is the purpose of all the gifts that the Holy Spirit has given to each of us? (See verse 7)

Just like the person with the matches not showing up affected the other three people, what do you think happens when you don't "show up" ready to use the gifts God has given you?

What gifts and abilities has God given you to use as a blessing for others?

DO
- Pull out a jar of peanut butter, butter knife, and piece of bread
- Choose a volunteer and ask if he or she is right or left handed.
- Have the volunteer place his dominate hand behind his back and attempt to spread the peanut butter onto the piece of bread using just one hand
- This will prove very difficult. As the child struggles, explain how God gave us two hands for a reason. Things are not as easy for us if we can only use one of the hands God gave us
- Next, ask the children who have shoes with laces to untie one of their shoes. (You can provide a laced shoe for any child who may not be in such footwear)
- After their shoes are untied, tell them to retie the shoe with one hand behind their back
- Again, this will prove very difficult. As it does, reiterate that God gave us two hands for a reason. Things are not as easy for us if we can only use one of the hands God gave us

FOLLOW UP
Ask: Did you know that the Bible says the people of the church are like a body? Why do you think the Bible says that?

Discuss with the children about how a body is made of many parts that all work together to get something done, so the church is made up of many people who should all be working together to get stuff done for Jesus.

Remind the children how hard it was trying to do things with just one hand. Likewise, the church can't do as a good a job when everyone is not pitching in and doing their part. It takes us *all* working together to get the job done.

FINISH UP

- Thank God for the gifts that He has given to you
- Ask God to show you how He wants you to use the gifts He has given to you

LESSON 34

SUPPLIES:
Several Legos, Lincoln Logs, or other connective/building toys

READ: 1 Peter 2:4-5

ENGAGE

Ants are tiny little creatures. So tiny, in fact, that it would take over 151,000 of them piled onto your bathroom scale to weigh even just one pound. Obviously, this shows that one ant by itself can't do very much!

But ants are rarely by themselves, are they? They are always with MANY of their buddies. In fact, there was once a group of scientists that discovered a colony of ants taking down a large ten-foot alligator! That's pretty impressive!

As Christians, we can be a lot like ants too. Maybe, by ourselves, we are small and can't do very much. But we shouldn't be by ourselves, should we? We should be joined together with others, so that we can take down Satan!

ASK

Who remembers how many ants it takes to weigh one pound?

Ready to do some math? Use the number of ants it takes to weigh one pound, then see how many ants it would take to weigh as much as you. (Teacher, you will most likely need to help with the math.)

Our Bible verses for today say that each Christian is like a stone in God's Temple. How impressive would a Temple be if it was made out of just one stone?

How many stones do you think it would take to make a Temple really big?

To be a stone in God's temple means you are involved in doing things for His kingdom. What things are you doing to help people know Jesus?

What are some things that you think you could do for Jesus this week?

DO

- Tell the children that you are going to build something really cool with Legos (or with whatever connective/building toy you have). Pull out one Lego and place it at the center of the table, then state, "There! Wow! What do you guys think? Cool, right?"
- When the class shows that they don't think it is so cool, ask them what is wrong
- The class will mostly likely say that you need to have many pieces to make something that is cool
- With that, bring out the whole box of Legos and divide them evenly between the kids. Go around and allow each person to add to your first piece.
- Keep going until all the pieces are used up. As each child is adding pieces, continue onto the FOLLOW UP

FOLLOW UP

Talk about how one ant sure can't take down a ten-foot alligator, and one Lego all by itself doesn't make much. Likewise, Christians by themselves can't do too much either. We need many Christians joined together to do something awesome for Jesus.

As the structure you are building gets bigger with each piece added, discuss things that a church can do when many people gather together—hold a VBS that needs many volunteers; have a church service with people ushering, greeting, praying, singing, playing instruments, preaching; gather cans of food for food drives; one person telling people about Jesus vs many people doing so, etc.

Finish by noting that it doesn't matter how old or young you are. Just as you can attach a brand new Lego piece to one that is ten years-old, so any Christian of any age can be part of something great at church!

FINISH UP

- Thank God for the chance to be part of His family and His Temple
- Ask God to use you to do great things for Him

LESSON 35

SUPPLIES:
List of people in the church who are in the hospital, in a nursing home, or shut-in; blank cards, colored pencils or crayons

READ: Acts 4:32-35

ENGAGE
Twelve year-old Johnny got a baseball glove for his birthday, and he was so excited for the chance to use it that he invited a bunch of friends over to play ball in his backyard. As they all played, Bobby, who had just moved into the neighborhood, stood in his own yard watching.

Noticing this, Johnny invited his new neighbor to join them. Bobby was super stoked that he got a chance to play. Afterwards, he told his parents how nice it was that Johnny invited him to play and even use the new glove. Bobby's parents were impressed and wanted to meet Johnny and his parents.

When they dropped by Johnny's house the next day, they ended up talking to Johnny's parents for a long time and were invited to church. That next Sunday, Bobby's parents did go to church, heard about Jesus, and decided to become Christians!

You see, one act of kindness can go a long way and make a great impact. When we act like Jesus, people notice!

ASK
What did Johnny do to make Bobby feel good?

What did that one act of kindness lead to?

What awesome things were the Christians in our Bible reading doing?

What were the great results of these awesome things?

God's people—the church—should be doing good things all the time, what good things have you done lately?

What good things can you do this week for others?

DO
- **Before class:** Get a list from your pastor, or pastoral care team, of people who are in the hospital, in a nursing home, or a shut-in
- After finishing the last question above, tell the children that you have something they can do right now to make a positive impact on someone's life
- Let them know about the list of people you have and their situations
- Instruct the children that they will each get a name of someone and will be able to make a card for them that will be mailed out, or delivered, this week
- Hand out blank cards to each child (or create cards from white sheets of paper)
- Allow the children to write encouraging notes and decorate the cards as they see fit
- As the children are doing this, move on to the FOLLOW UP

FOLLOW UP
Ask: Have you ever gotten a get well card or encouraging card from someone? How did it make you feel?

Talk about how just like Johnny's act of kindness made a big difference, so the card each child is creating can make a big difference as well.

As the children work to complete their cards, brainstorm other ways that each of you can be kind and encouraging this week.

FINISH UP

- Thank God for those who have done good things for you
- Ask God to show you who you can help this week
- Ask God to bless the cards so that each person who receives them will feel encouraged and loved

BONUS LESSON

SUPPLIES:
Heavy books or other heavy, stackable items

READ: Galatians 6:1-3

ENGAGE
Nine year-old Sam and his dad were going on a special backpacking trip one Saturday. Sam had been looking forward to it all week long—hiking with his dad, cooking over a fire, doing some fishing, and exploring for bears and deer.

When Saturday finally came, Sam could not have been more excited. However, about two hours into the hike, Sam really started to get tired. The backpack was getting very heavy, and the campground for lunch was still a couple miles down the trail. With his shoulders and back aching badly, Sam didn't know if he could make it.

Then, without saying a word, Dad grabbed Sam's backpack, swung it over his shoulders along with his own backpack, and carried it the rest of the way.

Sam sure felt a lot better with that weight off his shoulders!

ASK
What was Sam really excited about?

What caused Sam to lose some of that excitement?

What did Sam's dad do about this?

When the Bible says "share each other's burdens," it's not talking about backpacks. It's talking about helping people who are struggling or sad. Have you ever helped someone like that?

Has someone ever helped you when you were struggling or sad? How did it make you feel?

Being part of a church means helping people who are struggling. Do you know anyone that you could be helping?

Are you struggling or hurting for some reason? How can the church, or your family, help you?

DO
- Ask for a volunteer to come join you up front
- Tell this child to stick his arms straight out in front of him with his palms facing up
- After he has done so, place one large book across his forearms.
- Tell the class that this book represents a burden that (name of child) is carrying around with him
- Stack a second heavy book across the child's forearms
- After a moment or two, state that these books may not have seemed so heavy at first, but the longer that (name of child) has to hold them, the heavier the "burdens" become
- See how many books can be stacked before the volunteer cannot take any more "burdens"
- Allow for other volunteers if time permits

FOLLOW UP
Discuss how everyone has burdens and maybe, at first, they don't seem too bad or too heavy, just like Sam's backpack wasn't so heavy when he began to hike the trail and (name of child) didn't have too much trouble the first few seconds with the heavy book across his arms

Go on to talk about how the longer we try to hold our burdens by ourselves, the harder it becomes.

Ask: What should we do with our burdens so that they don't become too much for us?

Finish by talking about how important it is that we pray and give our burdens to God. We also need to share our burdens with parents and other adults who love and care for us. When we do that, then our burdens don't feel so heavy anymore

FINISH UP
- Thank God for people who can help carry your burdens
- Give any burdens you have over to the Lord
- Ask God to use you to help carry someone's burden

EPILOGUE

I hope God has truly blessed you as you have used this lesson book. I know He deeply desires to do so many awesome things in and through you. His plan for you, your family, and your ministry is truly remarkable! I trust you have grabbed hold of that.

If you, your family, or your class has been blessed in any way through these lessons, please do me the great favor of leaving a positive review on Amazon. Your review just may encourage another family to take this same journey.

I would also love to hear about what God has been doing through this lesson book in your home and/or classroom. Be sure to check my website www.markjmusser.com to contact me.

GOD BLESS YOU!

APPENDIX

1. http://www.kidssundayschool.com/324/gradeschool/sin-revealed.php
2. http://www.christianitycove.com/childrens-bible-lessons-god-wants-you-to-fasten-yourself-to-him-0307/829/
3. http://www.imaginefamilyministries.com/kidmin-themes--object-talks/gods-answers-prayer
4. http://www.sermons4kids.com/help_with_a_heavy_load_group_activities.htm

Printed in Great Britain
by Amazon